AF614223

誠 MAKOTO
e-zine for learners of Japanese

THEJAPANSHOP.COM
VOLUME 5 | ISSUE 47 | January 2022

ご購入(こうにゅう)
ありがとう
ございます。

Thank you so much
for your purchase!

あけましておめでとうございます！

Happy New Year!

Our first book of Japanese stories was about a legendary character named Hikoichi. I really loved how fun, wise, and mischievous he could be.

Last month, we introduced another Japanese traditional character similar to Hikoichi. His name is Kicchomu. By the way, although we simply write it in hiragana, his kanji is 吉四六(きっちょむ).

Like Hikoichi, Kicchomu thinks outside the box and is a little ずるい（sly; cunning; crafty). In this month's story, Kicchomu reminds us that things aren't always as they seem. We hope you will enjoy it.

Thank you!
Clay & Yumi

P.S. The cover has Kicchomu saying, 「あけおめ！」 This is short for... can you guess? あけましておめでとうございます (Congratulations on the New Year). You can take this two steps farther and say あけおめことよろ which is short for あけましておめでとう、今年もよろしくお願いします.

WHO ARE WE?

Nearly two decades ago, Clay & Yumi began **TheJapanesePage.com**, one of the Internet's oldest and largest ***free*** Japanese instructional sites with hundreds of free articles for beginners of Japanese.

They also maintain **TheJapanShop.com**, a web-store specializing in materials to help learners of Japanese.

Have any questions or comments? Contact us at **help@thejapanshop.com**

In this Issue:

LAUGHS, JOKES, RIDDLES, AND PUNS

ある人(ひと)が傘(かさ)をさして歩(ある)いていました。傘(かさ)は、とても小(ちい)さくて、ぼろぼろです。穴(あな)もたくさん開(あ)いていました。でも、その人(ひと)は全然(ぜんぜん)ぬれませんでした。どうしてでしょうか？

Scan for Recording

雨(あめ)が降(ふ)っていなかったからです。

One day, a person was walking with an umbrella. The umbrella was very small and tattered. It had many holes in it. But that person didn't get wet at all. Why is that?

Because it was not raining.

Vocabulary:

ジョーク *jo-ku*—a joke

ある人 *aru hito*—someone [ある (a certain; some) + 人(ひと) (person)]

が *ga*—(emphasizes the preceding word)

傘をさして *kasa o sashite*—with an umbrella up; with an open umbrella [て-form of 傘(かさ)をさす (hold an umbrella; put an umbrella up; 傘 (umbrella) + を (indicates 傘 as the direct object of action) + さす (to hold up; to put up; to raise)) which is used to connect to the next verb]

歩いていました *aruite imashita*—was walking [ていました form of 歩(ある)く (to walk) which is used to describe a continuous action happening in the past; how to form: Verb て-form + いました]

傘は *kasa wa*—the umbrella [傘 (umbrella) + は (indicates the sentence topic)]

とても *totemo*—very; exceedingly

小さくて *chiisakute*—small and [**て**-form of **小さい** (small; little) which is used to connect to the next phrase, creating the meaning of "and"; how to form: drop the ending **い** and add **くて**]

ぼろぼろ *boroboro*—worn-out; ragged; tattered

です *desu*—be; is

穴もたくさん開いていました *ana mo takusan aite imashita*—have many holes; there are many holes [**穴** (hole; hollow) + **も** (emphasizes the preceding word **穴**) + **たくさん** (many; lots; a lot) + **開いていました** (**ていました** form of **開く** (open; unclose; have a hole; form a gap); **ていました** is the polite past form of **ている** (is used to describe the actual condition or appearance of the subject); how to form: Verb **て**-form + **いました**)]

でも *demo*—but; however

その人は *sono hito wa*—that person [**その** (that; the) + **人** (person; people) + **は** (indicates the sentence topic)]

全然 *zenzen*—(not) at all; (not) in the slightest

ぬれませんでした *nuremasen deshita*—did not get wet [polite negative past form of **ぬれる** (to get wet); **でした** is a polite past tense marker]

どうして *doushite*—why; for what reason

でしょうか *deshou ka*—don't you think?; indicates question [polite (*teineigo*) language]

雨が降っていなかった *ame ga futte inakatta*—was not raining [**雨** (rain) + **が** (identifies what performs the action described by the verb) + **降っていなかった** (was not falling; plain negative past form of **降っている** (**ている**-form of **降る** (to fall (of rain, snow, ash, etc.); to come down) which is used to describe a continuous action or event; how to form: Verb **て**-form + **いる**); **~なかった** is the past tense negative plain form of verbs which adds the meaning of "did not do [verb]" to a sentence; how to form: V-**な~~い~~** + **かった**)]

から *kara*—because; since

VOCABULARY

Learn Useful Words, Phrases, and Sayings

Scan for Recording

耳(みみ)にたこができる

mimi ni tako ga dekiru

be sick and tired of hearing something; to hear something over and over again

Alternatively, if someone "talks your ears off," instead of using this idiom, you could ignore them while claiming your "ears are far" (*mimi ga tooi*) which means you can't hear too well.

Literally, "get calluses on one's ears." The "*tako*" here means "callus" such as what guitar players get on their fingers or the "corn" found on the feet of runners. Other common words with the same "*tako*" pronunciation are 1) 蛸 *tako* (octopus) and 2) 凧 *tako* (kite—the toy you fly in the sky). The Mexican food, taco, is pronounced タコス *takosu*.

EXAMPLE SENTENCE:

Example Sentence

「宿題(しゅくだい)をしなさい」と、耳(みみ)にたこができるほど母(はは)に言(い)われた。

shukudai o shinasai to, mimi ni tako ga dekiru hodo haha ni iwareta.

My mother said, "Do your homework!" so many times and I almost have calluses on my ears.

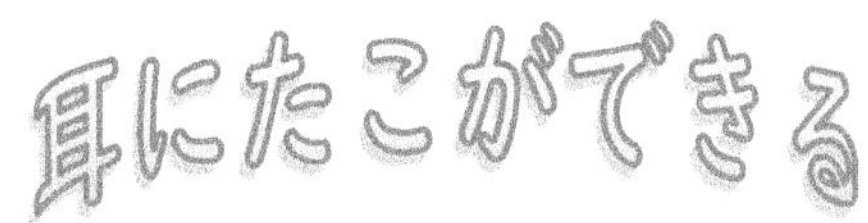

VOCABULARY

Learn Useful Words, Phrases, and Sayings

VOCABULARY:

宿題 *shukudai*—homework; assignment

を *o*—(direct object particle)

しなさい *shinasai*—do (your homework) [command form of する (to do) ; -*masu* stem form of verb (in this case, し) + なさい this is generally how a parent would speak to his or her child or a teacher would talk to students]

と *to*—(quotation marker) [quoting the preceding sentence]

母に *haha ni*—by (my) mother [母 (mother) + に (by)]

言われた *iwareta*—(I) was told [past of 言われる (be told), which is passive of 言う (to say)]

母 *haha*—mother

耳に *mimi ni*—on (my) ears [耳 (ear) + に (on)]

たこ *tako*—calluses

できる *dekiru*—to form; to develop

耳にたこができる *mimi ni tako ga dekiru*—be sick and tired of hearing something [used when hearing something over and over again to the point of getting sick and tired]

~ほど ~*hodo*—to the degree of; to extent that; almost that~

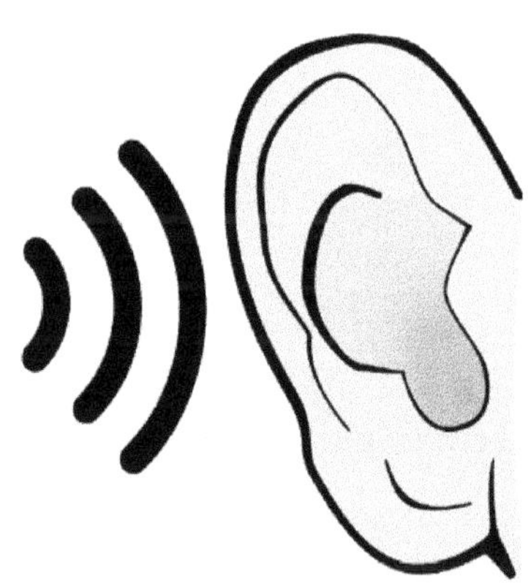

PREFECTURE SPOTLIGHT

Ishikawa 石川(いしかわ)

Japanese: 石川県 *ishikawa ken*
Capital: 金沢 Kanazawa
Population: 1,140,573 (October 31, 2019)

DID YOU KNOW?

Ishikawa prefecture has a mostly mountainous south, a narrow peninsula to the north, and a few islands. Kanazawa, its capital, has a metropolitan feel while richly preserving a traditional Japan of the past.

石川

PLACES TO SEE:

- **Kenrokuen**—one of Japan's three best gardens.
- **1000 Rice Fields—Senmaida**, found on the Noto Peninsula is a hillside with over a thousand rice fields.

- **Chaya district**—go back in time to enjoy traditional wooden houses and performances by geisha.
- With all its traditional crafts, Kanazawa is a great place to buy **unique Japanese gifts and souvenirs**.

FAMOUS FOR:

- **Traditional Japanese culture**—geisha, traditional art and crafts, old wooden buildings.
- **Kanazawa lacquerware**—high quality lacquerware decorated with gold dust.
- **Kanazawa gold leaf**—traditional craft of beating gold into ultra-thin sheets called *kinpaku.*
- **Wagashi**—famous for traditional candies still made the old fashioned way.

ごげん 語源 ETYMOLOGY

言葉の語源 *kotoba no gogen* – The origin of words:

Scan for Recording

ひも 紐 *Himo* (String)

紐【ヒモ】とは、自分は働かず、自分の付き合ってる女性に働かせてお金を貢がせる男のことを言います。ヒモの語源は、いろいろあるのですが、一番有力と言われているのが、海に潜って海産物をとる「海女さん」と、船に乗っている男の関係から来ているという説です。

海女さんは女性で、海に潜って働きます。海女さんは呼吸のために海の上に上がってきますが、その時に腰につけている紐をたぐって船に戻ります。船の上の男性は、紐を持って待っているだけなので、ヒモと呼ばれるようになったというわけです。

Himo (ヒモ) refers to a man who does not work, but makes the woman he is dating work to support him financially. There are various etymologies for the word "himo," but it is said that the most popular theory is that it comes from the relationship between "Ama-san", a woman who dives into the sea to collect marine products, and a man on the boat.

Continued

Ama-san is a woman who dives into the sea to work. She comes up from the sea to breathe, and at that time, she returns to the boat by pulling the string attached to her waist. The man on the boat just holds the string and waits for her, which is why he is referred to as "*himo.*"

Vocabulary

語源 etymology; origin of a word

紐とは *himo* is [紐 (*himo*; string; cord) + とは (describes the nature, content or state of an event or a thing)]

自分 myself; yourself; oneself; himself; herself

は (indicates the sentence topic)

働かず without working [from 働く (to work; to labor); ~ず means "without doing"; how to form: Verb (ない stem) ~~ない~~ + ず]

自分の one's; own [自分 (oneself; myself) + の ('s; indicates possessive)]

付き合ってる女性に働かせて make the woman (you are) dating work (to support you financially) [付き合ってる (in relationship; is dating; てる form of 付き合う (to go out with; to go steady with; to keep company with); てる is from ている which is used in conversation. In conversation, い is often dropped. It's called い抜き言葉 (*i-nuki kotoba*)) + 女性 (woman; female; feminine gender) + に (expresses the object of the verb) + 働かせて (make (someone) work; て-form of 働かせる (plain causative positive form of 働く (to work; to labor)) which is used to connect to the next phrase)]

お金を貢がせる make (her) give (him) money; make (her) give (him) financial aid [お金 (money) + を (indicates お金 as the direct object of action) + 貢がせる (make (someone) give; plain causative positive form of 貢ぐ (to give (in support); to supply (money)))]

男のこと all the things about the man [男 (man; guy) + のこと (all the things about; has a "focusing" feature and lets you know that the subject has a certain quality; how to form: Noun + のこと)]

Vocabulary Continued

言います refer (to a man who does not work) [ます-form of 言う (to call; to refer; to say)]

ヒモの語源は the etymology of *himo* [ヒモ (*himo*; string; cord) + の (of; for; modifier) + 語源 (etymology) + は (indicates the sentence topic)]

いろいろ various; variety of; all sorts of

ある to have; to be; to exist

のです (shows emphasis) [how to form: Verb (casual) + のです]

が but

一番有力 the most popular [一番 (most; number one; best) + 有力 (popular; prominent)]

と言われている it is said that; be said to be; be called [と (used for quoting (thoughts, speech, etc.)) + 言われている (be said; ている-form of 言う (to say; to call) which is used to describe a continuous action; how to form: Verb て-form + いる)]

の (verb nominalizer) [turns the preceding verb into a noun phrase]

が (emphasizes the preceding word)

海に潜って dive into the sea [海 (sea; ocean) + に (into; expresses direction and destination) + 潜って (て form of 潜る (to dive (into or under the water) which is used to connect to the next phrase))]

海産物をとる「海女さん」"Ama-san" who takes marine products [海産物 (marine products) + を (indicates the direct object of action) + とる (to take; to get; to acquire) +「海女 さん」("Ama-san"; 海女 (Ama) + さん (*san*; an honorific suffix which means Mr., Mrs., or Miss that can be used with both first and last names and both genders)); 「海産物をとる」is used to modify the noun 海女さん]

と and

船に乗っている be on a ship; on board the boat; on the boat [船 (ship; boat; watercraft) + に (on; expresses the location of existence) + 乗っている (ている-form of 乗る (to get on (ship, train, bus,

Vocabulary Continued

plane, etc.); to board) which is used to describe an ongoing action)]

船に乗っている男 a man on the boat [船に乗っている (on the boat) + 男 (man; male; guy)]

の関係 relationship of; relationship between [の (of; between; to; in) + 関係 (relationship; relation; connection; involvement)]

から来ている derive from; come from [から (from) + 来ている (ている-form of 来る (to come from; to derive from) which is used to describe a continuous action)]

という called; named; that; to define something; to emphasize something

説 theory; view

です be; is

女性で is a woman and [女性 (woman; female; feminine gender) + で (て-form of です (be; is) which is used to connect to the next phrase, creating the meaning of "and")]

海に潜って働きます dive into the sea to work [海 (sea; ocean) + に (into; expresses the direction and destination) + 潜って (て-form of 潜る (to dive (into or under the water); to go under) which is used to connect to the next verb 働きます) + 働きます (ます-form of 働く (to work; to labor))]

呼吸のために for breathing [呼吸 (breathing; respiration) + のために (for; in order to; for the benefit of); how to form: Noun + のために]

海の上に上がってきます come up to the sea; go up on the sea [海 (sea; ocean; waters) + の上に (above and beyond; on the top of; on; onto; over) + 上がってきます (come up; from 上がる (to go up; to come up); ~てきます is used to describe a motion coming towards the place where the speaker is; how to form: Verb て-form + きます)]

が and [conjunction; is used to combine two sentences together into one compound sentence]

その時に at that time; on that occasion; at that moment [その時 (at that time) + に (specifies the time)]

腰につけている紐 the string attached to (her) waist [腰 (waist; lower back; hips) + に (to) + つけている (ている form of つける (to attach; to join; to fasten) which is used to describe the appearance of the subject) + 紐 (string; cord); 「腰につけている」is used to modify the noun 紐]

Vocabulary Continued

腰につけている紐をたぐって by pulling the string attached to (her) waist [腰につけている紐 (the string attached to (her) waist) + を (indicates the direct object of action) + たぐって (by pulling; て-form of たぐる (to pull in; to draw in) which is used to express a means for a subsequent action)]

船に戻ります return to the boat [船 (boat; ship; watercraft) + に (to; expresses direction and destination) + 戻ります (ます-form of 戻る (to return; to go back))]

船の上の男性は the man on the boat [船 (boat; ship; watercraft) + の (is used to tell location) + 上 (top; surface; above; up) + の (modifier) + 男性 (man; male; masculine gender) + は (indicates the sentence topic)]

紐を持って hold the string and [紐 (string; cord) + を (indicates the direct object of action) + 持って (hold and; て-form of 持つ (to hold (in one's hand); to carry) which is used to connect to the next phrase, creating the meaning of "and")]

待っている is/are waiting; awaiting; wait [ている-form of 待つ (to wait) which is used to describe an ongoing action]

だけなので because (he's) just; because only [だけ (just; only) + な (is added because the preceding word だけ is actually from the noun 丈 (たけ length)) + ので (because of ...; so; since; given that; expresses reason or cause); how to form: Noun / な-adjective + な + ので]

ヒモと呼ばれる be referred to as "*himo*" [ヒモ (*himo*; string; cord) + と呼ばれる (be referred to as; be known and described as; be called; と (used for quoting (thoughts, speech, etc.)) + 呼ばれる (plain passive positive form of 呼ぶ (to call; to designate)))]

ようになった came to be that [plain past form of ようになる (to come to be that; to reach the point that; to turn into ~; how to form: Verb (dictionary / ない form) + ようになる)]

というわけです which is why; that's why; no wonder; this means; it is the case that ~ [how to form: Phrase + というわけです]

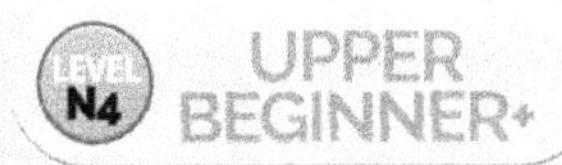

ANIME / MANGA PHRASE

Surprise your Japanese friends with these phrases

Please see the sound files for the pronunciation

ぼく　しんせかい　かみ

「僕は新世界の神になる」

やがみライト

八神月のセリフ・デスノートより

Scan for Recording

「boku wa shin sekai no kami ni naru」 yagami raito no serifu / desunooto yori

"I'll be the god of the new world"
Line from Yagami Light From "Death Note"

VOCABULARY

「」—(quotation marks; " ")

僕 *boku*—I; me [male term or language]

は *wa*—(indicates the sentence topic)

新世界の神 *shin sekai no kami*—god of the new world [新(しん) (new) + 世界(せかい) (world) + の (of; modifier) + 神(かみ) (god; deity)]

になる *ni naru*—become; turn out; come to [how to form: Noun + になる]

八神月のセリフ *yagami raito no serifu*—line from Yagami Light [八神月 (Yagami Light) + の (from; of; modifier) + セリフ (one's lines; speech; words)]

デスノートより *desunooto yori*—from "Death Note" [デスノート (Death Note) + より (from)]

HAIKU

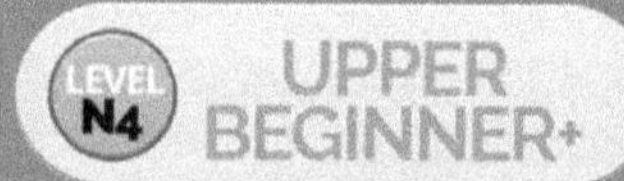

Condensed Japanese Language and Culture

Masaoka Shiki 正岡子規

初日(はつひ)さす　硯(すずり)の海(うみ)に

波(なみ)もなし

Haiku Audio

hatsuhi sasu / suzuri no umi ni / nami mo nashi

The first sunrise of the year shines /
and on the inkstone ocean /
there are no waves

Explanation

Explanation:

初日(はつひ)がさす墨(すみ)の海(うみ)は、とてもおだやかで波(なみ)が立(た)っていません。

The first sunrise of the year lights the ocean of ink which is very peaceful and free of waves.

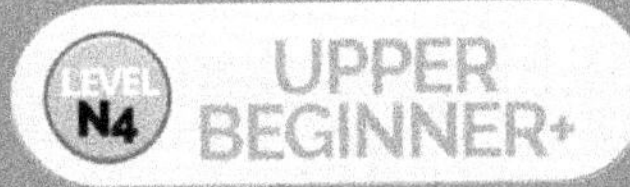

Continued

Vocabulary

初日 new year's day sunrise; first day; opening day; first sunrise of the year

さす to shine (of the sun); to light

硯の海に in the ocean of the ink slab [硯(すずり) (ink slab; inkstone) + の (of; modifier) + 海(うみ) (ocean; sea) + に (in; expresses location of existence)]

波もなし there are no waves [波(なみ) (wave) + も (emphasizes the preceding word 波(なみ)) + なし (without; none)]

初日さす the first sunrise of the year lights (the ocean) [初日(はつひ) (first sunrise of the year) + さす (to shine; to light)]

墨の海 ocean of the ink [墨(すみ) (ink; *sumi*) + の (of; modifier) + 海(うみ) (ocean; sea)]

は (indicates the sentence topic)

とても very; exceedingly

おだやかで is peaceful and [おだやか (peaceful; calm; mild; quiet; gentle) + で (and; て-form of です (be; is) which is used to connect to the next phrase, creating the meaning of "and")]

波が立っていません free of waves; there are no waves; waves are not rising [波(なみ) (wave) + が (identifies what performs the action) + 立(た)っていません (is/are not rising; polite negative form of 立(た)っている (is/are rising; ている-form of 立つ (to stand; to rise) which is used to describe the actual condition or appearance of the subject); how to form: Verb て-form + いません)]

正岡子規 Masaoka Shiki (1867-1902) [was a Japanese poet, author, and literary critic in Meiji period. He emphasized creativity within the individual and ultimately established haiku poetry as modern literature.]

KANJI SPOTLIGHT

Learning kanji one character at a time.

LEVEL BEGINNER JLPT N5

JLPT N5 Kanji

On: フ

Kun: ちち　とう

Meaning: father

Hint: It looks like a father tying his tie.

Audio of Readings

Stroke Order:

父 ノ ハ ソ 父

Examples:

お父(とう)さん a father

父(ちち)の日(ひ) Father's Day

仕事(しごと)が終(お)わったら、お父(とう)さんはテレビの前(まえ)でごろごろします。

shigoto ga owattara, otousan wa terebi no mae de gorogoro shimasu.

After work, dad just loafs around in front of the TV.

[The honorific "o" is usually added to *tousan*.]

Audio of Example

VOCABULARY:

仕事 *shigoto*—work; job; task; employment

が *ga*—(identifies what performs the action described by the verb 終(お)わった

JLPT N5 Kanji

On: フ

Kun: ちち　とう

Meaning: father

Hint: It looks like a father tying his tie.

Audio of Readings

Vocabulary Continued

ら; emphasizes the preceding word 仕事(しごと))

終わったら *owattara*—after (work); when (you're) done; when (you) finish [from 終(お)わる (to finish; to end); ~たら is a conditional form. It can express a time sequence like "after/when" and conditions like "if". How to form: Verb (た form) + ら]

お父さん *otousan*—father; dad; papa; pa [お is honorific/polite/humble prefix]

は *wa*—(topic marker particle)

テレビの前 *terebi no mae*—in front of the TV [テレビ (TV; television) + の (of; modifier) + 前 (in front; before (e.g. a building))]

で *de*—at; in [indicates the location of action]

ごろごろします *gorogoro shimasu*—to loaf around; to idle away [ごろごろ (idleness; idling about) + します (ます form of する (to do))]

V+前(まえ)に・N+の前(まえ)に

ABOUT:

前(まえ)に can be used both spatially and temporally.

In front of something (spatially) and ***previous*** to something (temporally).

HOW TO USE:

■ **Verb**: Place after the plain, non-past verb.

■ **Noun**: Place の前(まえ) after the noun.

EXAMPLES:

食(た)べる<u>前(まえ)に</u>、手(て)を洗(あら)ってください。

Please wash your hands **<u>before</u>** eating.

[eating | before | hand | wash | please]

Example 1

仕事(しごと)に行(い)く<u>前(まえ)に</u>、朝(あさ)ごはんを食(た)べます。

<u>Before</u> going to work, (I) eat breakfast.

[work | to | go | before | breakfast | eat]

Example 2

Continued

VOCABULARY:

食べる *taberu*—to eat

前に *mae ni*—before; earlier; previously; in front of~

手を洗ってください *te o aratte kudasai*—please wash (your) hands [from 手を洗う (wash one's hands; 手 (hand; arm) + を (indicates 手 as the direct object of action) + 洗う (to wash; to cleanse)); ~てください means "please do" which is used when requesting, instructing, ordering someone to do something; how to form: Verb (て form) + ください]

仕事に行く *shigoto ni iku*—go to work; report to work [仕事 (work; job; occupation; employment) + に (to; expresses direction and destination with the motion verb 行く) + 行く (to go)]

朝ごはん *asagohan*—breakfast

を *o*—(indicates the direct object of action)

食べます *tabemasu*—to eat [ます-form of 食べる (to eat)]

よんでみよう！LET'S READ!

Learn through reading for (very) beginners of Japanese

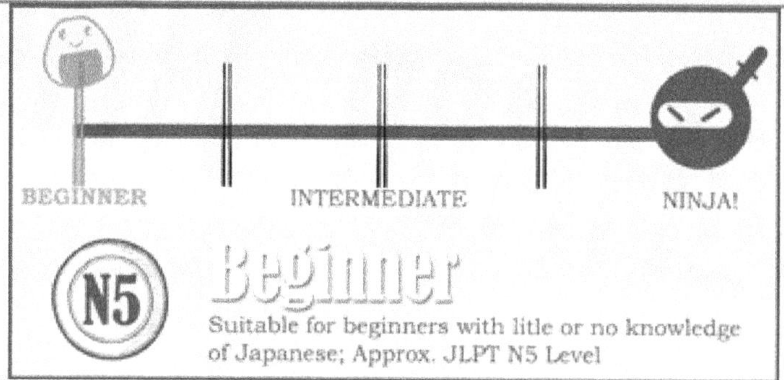

Have you only recently learned hiragana but need practice? Or perhaps, your hiragana is no problem, but you want to build your reading comprehension?

This segment is here to the rescue!

Read real Japanese—beginner level but not boring Japanese! Enjoy reading flash fiction, super short essays, and funny stories of common mistakes made by foreigners in Japan.

Best of all, the only requirement is that you can read hiragana. Vocabulary and grammar will be defined and explained.

The format is a little different from our other more advanced readers. The idea is for the reader to read the entire story three times. Each page will have a sentence or two in hiragana (with spaces between words for you to see "words" instead of syllables) at the top and that same content in full Japanese (with furigana) at the bottom. The middle will have the glossary and grammatical explanations. Lastly, the story will be presented in Japanese without furigana. See if you can read it after going through the explanations.

If you have just learned hiragana, you may want to listen to the sound file while reading the hiragana section to practice correct pronunciation. If you have studied Japanese a bit longer, you may want to start with the bottom version and take note of the glossary for understanding.

Makoto+ members can access this in a more interactive format. To learn more:
http://MakotoPlus.com

And now...

Let's learn about...

COUNTRYSIDE IN JAPAN

Normal Speed

Slow Speed

The top and bottom Japanese texts are identical in meaning. The top version is only in hiragana and includes spaces between words. The bottom version has no spaces and uses kanji with furigana. Unless you are just practicing hiragana recognition, try to work through both versions. Scan the QR codes for the sound files.

Normal Speed

Slow Speed

日本(にほん)の田舎(いなか)

COUNTRYSIDE IN JAPAN

にほん　は、とても　あんぜんな　くに　です。どろぼう　や　さつじん　など　は　あまり　おこりません。

GLOSSARY AND NOTES

日本の田舎 *nihon no inaka*—Japanese countryside; rural of Japan; countryside in Japan [日本(にほん) (Japan) + の (of; in; modifier) + 田舎(いなか) (countryside; rural area)]

は *wa*—(indicates the sentence topic)

とても安全な国 *totemo anzenna kuni*—very safe country [とても (very; exceedingly) + 安全(あんぜん)な (safe; secure; risk-free) + 国(くに) (country; state)]

です *desu*—be; is

泥棒や殺人などは *dorobou ya satsujin nado wa*—theft, murder, etc. [泥棒 (theft; robbery; burglar; thief) + や (and; or; connecting particle; is used to separate similar nouns) + 殺人 (murder; homicide; manslaughter) + など (and so on; etc.) + は (indicates the sentence topic); ~や~など is used to list objects and contains the meaning of "there are other similar things"]

あまり起こりません *amari okorimasen*—barely happen; do not happen very often [あまり ((not) very; (not) much) + 起(お)こりません (do not happen; polite negative form of 起(お)こる (to occur; to happen)); あまり~ない means "not very ~; not much ~; barely ~"; how to form: あまり + Verb (negative form)]

日本(にほん)は、とても安全(あんぜん)な国(くに)です。泥棒(どろぼう)や殺人(さつじん)などはあまり起(お)こりません。

その　せい　か、がいこくじん　が　とても　おどろく　しゅうかん　が　あります。それ　は、やさい　の　むじん　はんばい　です。のうか　の　ひと　は、ちいさな　こや　の　なか　に　やさい　を　ならべます。

GLOSSARY AND NOTES

そのせいか *sono sei ka*—perhaps because of that [その (that; the) + せいか (perhaps because ~; it may be because)]

外国人 *gaikokujin*—foreigner; alien; foreign citizen [外 (outside; exterior) + 国 (country; state) + 人 (person; people)]

が *ga*—(emphasizes the preceding word 外国人)

とても驚く習慣があります *totemo odoroku shuukan ga arimasu*—there is a custom that is surprising (to foreigners) [とても (very; exceedingly) + 驚く (to be surprised; feel astonished; is used to modify the noun 習慣) + 習慣 (custom; habitual practice) + (が)あります (there is/are (non-living things); how to form: Noun + (が)あります)]

それは *sore wa*—that is [それ (that; it) + は (indicates the sentence topic)]

野菜の無人販売 *yasai no mujin hanbai*—unmanned selling of vegetables [野菜 (vegetable) + の (of; modifier) + 無人 (unmanned; unattended) + 販売 (selling; marketing)]

農家の人は *nouka no hito wa*—the farmer [農家 (farmer; farming family) + の (modifier) + 人 (person; people) + は (indicates the sentence topic)]

小さな *chiisana*—small; little; tiny

小屋の中に *koya no naka ni*—in (small) hut; inside the hut [小屋 (hut; cabin; shed) + の (modifier) + 中 (inside; in; interior) + に (expresses the location of existence)]

野菜を並べます *yasai o narabemasu*—set up the vegetables [野菜 (vegetable) + を (indicates 野菜 as the direct object of action) + 並べます (ます-form of 並べる (to set up; to line up))]

そのせいか、外国人がとても驚く習慣があります。それは、野菜の無人販売です。農家の人は、小さな小屋の中に野菜を並べます。

やさい　を　かいたい　ひとは、すきな　やさい　を　とって、おかね　を　はこ　に　いれます。ねだん　は　よこ　に　かいて　おきます。たとえば、「いっこ　ひゃく　えん」。

GLOSSARY AND NOTES

野菜を買いたい人は *yasai o kaitai hito wa*—as for a person who wants to buy vegetables [野菜(やさい) (vegetable) + を (marks 野菜(やさい) as the direct object) + 買(か)いたい (want to buy; from 買(か)う (to buy; to purchase); ~たい means "want to do something"; how to form: Verb ~~ます~~ (stem form) + たい) + 人(ひと) (person) + は (topic marker)]

好きな *sukina*—chosen; preferred; (you) want; (one's) favorite

野菜を取って *yasai o totte*—take the vegetable (you want) and [野菜(やさい) (vegetable) + を (indicates 野菜(やさい) as the direct object of action) + 取(と)って (take and; て-form of 取る (to take; to pick up) which is used to connect to the next phrase, creating the meaning of "and")]

お金を箱に入れます *okane o hako ni iremasu*—put the money in the box [お金 (money) + を (indicates お金(かね) as the direct object of action) + 箱(はこ) (box; chest; case) + に (in) + 入(い)れます (ます-form of 入(い)れる (to put in))]

値段は *nedan wa*—the price [値段(ねだん) (price; cost) + は (indicates the sentence topic)]

横に書いておきます *yoko ni kaite okimasu*—to write the (price) beside (the vegetable on purpose so that someone else can refer to it later) [横(よこ) (side; beside; next to) + に (expresses the location of existence) + 書(か)いておきます (from 書(か)く (to write); ~ておきます is used when you focus on the future use; how to use: Verb て-form + おきます)]

たとえば *tatoeba*—for example; for instance; e.g.

「」—(quotation marks; " ")

1個百円 *ikko hyaku en*—one hundred yen per piece [1個(いっこ) (one piece; 個(こ) is a counter for articles) + 百円(ひゃくえん) (one hundred yen; 百(ひゃく) (hundred) + 円(えん) (yen; Japanese monetary unit))]

野菜(やさい)を買(か)いたい人(ひと)は、好(す)きな野菜(やさい)を取(と)って、お金(かね)を箱(はこ)に入(い)れます。値段(ねだん)は横(よこ)に書(か)いておきます。たとえば、「1個(いっこ)百(ひゃく)円(えん)」。

だれ　も　おかね　を　ぬすみません。だれ　も　やさい　を　ぬすみません。にほん　の　いなか　は、とても　あんぜん　で　へいわです。

GLOSSARY AND NOTES

だれもお金を盗みません *dare mo okane o nusumimasen*—no one steals the money [だれも (no one; nobody) + お金(かね) (money) + を (indicates the direct object of action) + 盗(ぬす)みません (do not steal; polite negative form of 盗(ぬす)む (to steal))]

だれも野菜を盗みません *dare mo yasai o nusumimasen*—no one steals the vegetables [だれも (no one; nobody) + 野菜(やさい) (vegetable) + を (indicates the direct object of action) + 盗(ぬす)みません (do not steal; polite negative form of 盗(ぬす)む (to steal))]

日本の田舎 *nihon no inaka*—Japanese countryside; rural of Japan; countryside in Japan [日本(にほん) (Japan) + の (of; in; modifier) + 田舎(いなか) (countryside; rural area)]

とても安全で平和 *totemo anzen de heiwa*—very safe and peaceful [とても (very; exceedingly) + 安全(あんぜん) (safe; safety; security) + で (and; て-form of です (be; is) which is used to connect to the next phrase, creating the meaning of "and") + 平和(へいわ) (peaceful; peace; harmony)]

だれもお金(かね)を盗(ぬす)みません。だれも野菜(やさい)を盗(ぬす)みません。日本(にほん)の田舎(いなか)は、とても安全(あんぜん)で平和(へいわ)です。

日本の田舎

COUNTRYSIDE IN JAPAN

Normal Speed

Now, let's read the story once more in natural Japanese.
Lastly, check the English translation to make sure you understand.

Slow Speed

日本は、とても安全な国です。泥棒や殺人などはあまり起こりません。そのせいか、外国人がとても驚く習慣があります。それは、野菜の無人販売です。農家の人は、小さな小屋の中に野菜を並べます。野菜を買いたい人は、好きな野菜を取って、お金を箱に入れます。値段は横に書いておきます。たとえば、「1個百円」。だれもお金を盗みません。だれも野菜を盗みません。日本の田舎は、とても安全で平和です。

ENGLISH: (try to save this for last)

Japan is a very safe country. Theft, murder, etc. barely happen. Perhaps because of that, there is a custom that is very surprising to foreigners. It is the unmanned selling of vegetables. Farmers set up their vegetables in small huts. If anyone wants to buy vegetables, they can take any vegetable they want and put the money in the box. The price is written beside the vegetable. For example, "One hundred yen per vegetable". No one will steal the money. No one will steal the vegetables. The countryside in Japan is very safe and peaceful.

KEY VOCABULARY

日本の田舎 *nihon no inaka*—Japanese countryside; rural of Japan; countryside in Japan [日本 (Japan) + の (of; in; modifier) + 田舎 (countryside; rural area)]

とても安全で平和 *totemo anzen de heiwa*—very safe and peaceful [とても (very; exceedingly) + 安全 (safe; safety; security) + で (and; て-form of です (be; is) which is used to connect to the next phrase, creating the meaning of "and") + 平和 (peaceful; peace; harmony)]

野菜の無人販売 *yasai no mujin hanbai*—unmanned selling of vegetables [野菜 (vegetable) + の (of; modifier) + 無人 (unmanned; unattended) + 販売 (selling; marketing)]

外国人 *gaikokujin*—foreigner

値段 *nedan*—price

誰でも *dare demo*—anyone; anybody; whoever

だれも *dare mo*—no one; nobody

JAPANESE READER

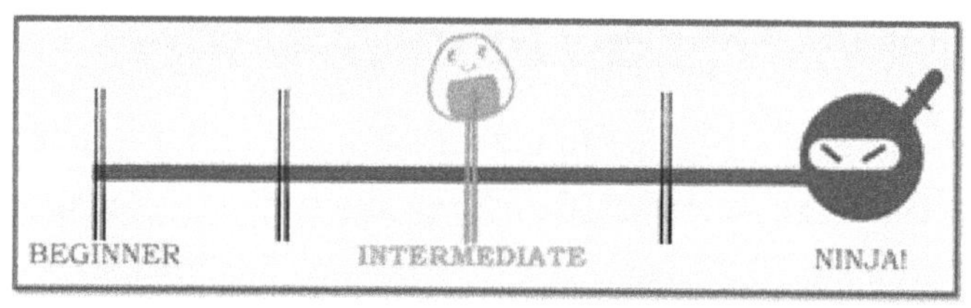

きっちょむさんのネズミの彫(ほ)り物(もの)
Kicchomu's Mouse Carving

Story Read Normal Speed

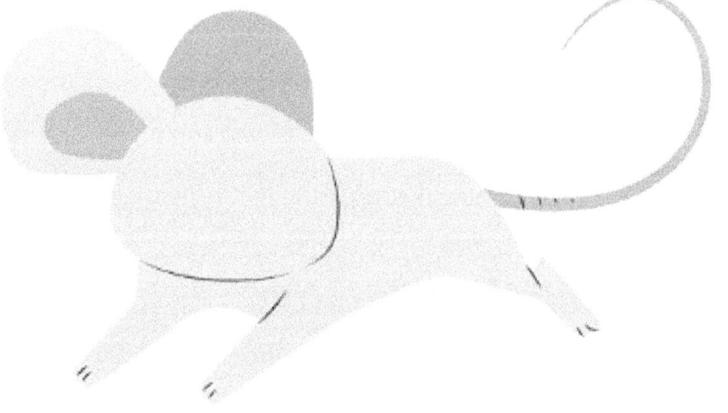

Story Read Slow Speed

Work through the story, sentence-by-sentence, referring to the vocabulary and grammar explanations below as needed.

きっちょむさんのネズミの彫(ほ)り物(もの)

むかしむかし、きっちょむさんという面白(おもしろ)い人(ひと)がいました。

ある日(ひ)、庄屋(しょうや)さんがきっちょむさんを家(いえ)に呼(よ)びました。

きっちょむさんのネズミの彫り物 Kicchomu's mouse carving [きっちょむさん (Kicchomu; さん is an honorific suffix which means Mr., Mrs., or Miss that can be used with both first and last names and both genders) + の ('s; indicates possessive) + ネズミ (mouse; rat) + の (of; modifier) + 彫(ほ)り物(もの) (carving; engraving; sculpture)]

むかしむかし long ago; once upon a time

きっちょむさんという named Kicchomu [きっちょむさん (Kicchomu) + という (named; is used to define, describe, and generally just talk about the thing itself)]

面白い人 interesting man [面白(おもしろ)い (interesting; fascinating; enthralling) + 人(ひと) (man; person; people)]

(が)いました there was/were [polite past form of (が)いる (there is/are; to be (living things)); how to form: Noun + (が)いました]

ある日 one day; (on) a certain day [ある (a certain; some) + 日(ひ) (day)]

庄屋(しょうや)さんが the village headman [庄屋 (village headman) + さん (politeness marker; is used after a noun or sometimes な-adjective) + が (identifies who performs the action)]

きっちょむさんを家に呼びました called Kicchomu to (his) house [きっちょむさん (Kicchomu) + を (indicates the direct object of action) + 家(うち) (house; dwelling; residence) + に (to; expresses direction and destination) + 呼(よ)びました (called; polite past form of 呼(よ)ぶ (to call; to invite))]

庄屋(しょうや)さんは、お金持(かねも)ちでいつも自慢(じまん)ばかりしているので、きっちょむさんは庄屋(しょうや)さんのことがあまり好(す)きではありません。

庄屋(しょうや)さんは、きっちょむさんが来(く)ると、嬉(うれ)しそうにまた自慢話(じまんばなし)を始(はじ)めました。

庄屋さんは the village headman [庄屋さん (village headman) + は (indicates the sentence topic)]

お金持(かねも)ちで rich and [お金持ち (rich person; rich; wealthy) + で (and; て-form of です (be; is) which is used to connect to the next phrase, creating the meaning of "and")]

いつも always; all the time; at all times

自慢ばかりしている do/does nothing but brag [自慢(じまん) (pride; boast; brag; boasting; bragging; self-praise) + ばかり (only; just (something); nothing but) + している (ている-form of する (to do) which is used to describe one's habitual actions)]

ので so; because of ...; since; given that [expresses reason or cause]

庄屋さんのこと all the things about the village headman [庄屋さん (village headman) + のこと (all the things about; it has a "focusing" feature and lets you know that the subject has a certain quality; how to form: Noun + のこと)]

庄屋さんのことがあまり好きではありません (Kicchomu) doesn't like all the things about the village headman very much; (Kicchomu) doesn't really like the village headman [庄屋さんのこと (all the things about the village headman) + が (emphasizes the preceding word) + あまり ((not) very; (not) much) + 好きではありません (doesn't/don't like; not liking; polite negative form of 好き (to one's liking; being fond of; liking; like; want)); あまり~ない means "not very ~; not much ~; barely ~"; how to form: あまり + な adjective + ~~な~~ではありません]

きっちょむさんが来ると when Kicchomu comes [きっちょむさん (Kicchomu) + が (identifies who performs the action described by the verb 来る) + 来る (to come; to arrive) + と (when; whenever [A] happens, [B] also happens; how to form: Verb (dictionary / ない form) + と)]

嬉(うれ)しそうに happily; joyfully; delightedly [嬉しそう (delightful; glad-looking) + に (is added to 嬉しそう in order to turn it into an adverbial phrase)]

また again; once more; once again; also

自慢話を始めました started bragging; started boastful speech [自慢話(じまんばなし) (bragging; boastful speech) + を (indicates the direct object of action) + 始めました (started; polite past form of 始(はじ)める (to start; to begin))]

「最近、たいへんな彫り物の名人にお願いして、これをつくってもらったよ。」と言って、出してきたのは、ネズミの彫り物でした。

「」(quotation marks; " ")

最近 recently; lately; these days

たいへんな very; great; immense

彫り物の名人 master at carving; expert of carving [彫り物 (carving; sculpture; engraving) + の (of; at; modifier) + 名人 (master; expert)]

彫り物の名人にお願いして ask a great master at carving [彫り物の名人 (master at carving) + に (expresses the object of the verb) + お願いして (ask; て-form of お願いする (ask; ask a favor of) which is used to connect to the next phrase)]

これをつくってもらった made this for (me) [これ (this; this one) + を (indicates the direct object of action) + つくってもらった (from つくる (to make; to build; to produce); ~てもらった is the plain past form of てもらう (to get somebody to do something; request a favor); how to form: Verb て form + もらった)]

よ (sentence ender showing emphasis and certainty)

と言って出してきた said and brought out; said and showed [と (quotation marker) + 言って (said and; て-form of 言う (to say; to utter) which is used to connect to the next verb 出してきた, creating the meaning of "and") + 出してきた (took out something and brought it to the place where the speaker is; from 出す (to take out; to put out; to show; to reveal); ~てきた is the plain past form of ~てくる (describes a motion coming towards the place where the speaker is); how to form: Verb て form + きた)]

出してきたのはネズミの彫り物でした what the (village headman) brought out was a mouse carving [出してきた (brought out; is used to modify the placeholder の) + の (a nominalizer that acts like a noun; placeholder for nouns) + は (indicates the sentence topic) + ネズミの彫り物 (mouse carving; carving of a mouse) + でした (was/were; a polite past tense marker, typically used with nouns and な-adjectives; how to form: Noun / な-adjective (stem form) + でした)]

「ほら、このネズミは、まるで、生きているみたいだろう？」と言って、にやにやしています。きっちょむさんは、ネズミの彫り物をじっと見てから、こう言いました。「庄屋さん、確かにこのネズミはよくできています。

ほら look; see; here; hey

このネズミ this mouse [この (this; these) + ネズミ (mouse; rat)]

まるで just like; as though; as if

生きているみたい (this mouse) looks like it's alive [生きている (alive; living; live; in-life; ている form of 生きる (to live) which is used to describe the appearance of the subject; how to form: Verb て-form + いる) + みたい (it looks like; it seems like; is used to express your opinion, assumption based on what you have seen; how to form: Verb (casual) + みたい)]

だろう？ doesn't it?; right?; don't you agree?

と言って say and [と (quotation marker) + 言って (say and; て-form of 言う (to say; to utter) which is used to connect to the next verb, creating the meaning of "and")]

にやにやしています (he is) grinning; he grins [ています-form of にやにやする (grin; smirk) which is used to describe an ongoing action; how to form: Verb て form + います]

ネズミの彫り物をじっと見てから after staring at the mouse carving [ネズミの彫り物 (mouse carving) + を (indicates the direct object of action) + じっと見てから (after staring; from じっと見る (to stare; to watch steadily); じっと (motionlessly (e.g. stand, wait); (be) still) + 見る (to see; to look; to watch); ~てから means "after doing (verb)..."; how to form: Verb て-form + から)]

こう言いました said; said so [polite past form of こう言う (say so); こう (refers to what the speaker has said) + 言いました (polite past form of 言う (to say; to utter))]

確かに surely; certainly; for certain; of course; evidently

このネズミは this mouse [この (this) + ネズミ (mouse; rat) + は (indicates the sentence topic)]

よくできています well-made; very good [よく (well; skillfully; nicely; properly) + できています (ています-form of できる (to be made; to be built) which is used to describe the actual condition of appearance of the subject; how to form: Verb て-form + います)]

でも、私はもっとうまく作れます。明日までに作ってお見せしましょう。」

次の日、きっちょむさんは、自分で作ったネズミの彫り物を持って庄屋さんの家に行きました。

でも but; however

私 I; me

もっとうまく作れます (I) can make a better (one) [もっと (even more; (some) more) + うまく (well; skillfully; successfully) + 作れます (can make; polite potential positive form of 作る (to make; to build; to produce))]

明日までに by tomorrow [明日 (tomorrow) + まで (until; till; up to) + に (is used to specify time)]

作ってお見せしましょう (I'll) make and show [作って (make and; て-form of 作る (to make; to produce) which is used to connect to the next verb, creating the meaning of "and") + お見せしましょう((I'll) show; polite volitional from 見せる (to show; to display) which is used when the speaker initiates an act; how to form: ~ます → ~ましょう; お is an honorific/polite/humble prefix)]

次の日 the next day; the following day [次 (next; following; subsequent) + の (modifier) + 日 (day; days)]

自分で by oneself; by myself; on your own; by yourself [自分 (myself; yourself; oneself; himself; herself) + で (by; indicates a means or method)]

作ったネズミの彫り物を持って take the mouse carving which (he) made [作った (made; plain past form of 作る (to make)) + ネズミの彫り物 (mouse carving; carving of a mouse) + を (indicates the direct object of action) + 持って (て-form of 持つ (to take; to hold (in one's hand); to carry) which is used to connect to the next phrase)]

庄屋さんの家に行きました went to the village headman's house [庄屋さん (village headman) + の ('s; of; indicates possessive) + 家 (house; residence; dwelling) + に (to; expresses direction and destination) + 行きました (went; polite past form of 行く (to go))]

そして、庄屋さんに自分の作ったネズミの彫り物を見せました。一晩で作ったきっちょむさんのネズミは不細工で、どう見てもネズミには見えません。

そして and; and then

庄屋さんに to the village headman [庄屋さん (village headman) + に (to)]

自分の作ったネズミの彫り物を見せました showed the mouse carving which (he) made (himself); showed the mouse carving of (his) own making [自分 (himself; herself; oneself; myself; yourself) + の ('s; of; modifier) + 作った (made; plain past form of 作る (to make)) + ネズミの彫り物 (mouse carving; carving of a mouse) + を (indicates the direct object of action) + 見せました (showed; polite past form of 見せる (to show; to display))]

一晩で in a night; in one night; overnight [一晩 (one night; overnight; all night; one evening) + で (in; at; indicates time of action)]

一晩で作ったきっちょむさんのネズミ Kicchomu's mouse which he made overnight [一晩で (overnight) + 作った (made; plain past form of 作る (to make)) + きっちょむさん (Kicchomu) + の ('s; of; indicates possessive) + ネズミ (mouse; rat)]

不細工で ugly and [不細工 (ugly; poorly made; unattractive) + で (and; て-form of です (be; is) which is used to connect to the next phrase, creating the meaning of "and")]

どう見ても no matter how you look at it; anyway you look at it; from any point of view [どう (how) + 見ても (from 見る (to see; to look; to view); ~ても means "no matter how ~" which is used when the opposite result happens (or opposite action is taken) to what people normally expected; how to form: Verb て-form + も)]

ネズミには見えません (it) doesn't look like a mouse [ネズミ (mouse; rat) + には (puts more emphasis and restriction on the preceding word ネズミ) + 見えません (doesn't/don't look like; polite negative form of 見える (to look; to appear; to seem))]

一方、庄屋さんのネズミは、名人が作ったもので、本物そっくりです。「きっちょむさん、どう見ても私のネズミのほうが本物に見えるぞ。」きっちょむさんは、首を横に振ってこう言いました。

一方 on the other hand; on the one hand

庄屋さんのネズミ the village headman's mouse [庄屋さん (village headman) + の ('s; of; indicates possessive) + ネズミ (mouse; rat)]

名人が作ったもので because (it) was made by a master [名人 (master; expert) + が (emphasizes the preceding word 名人) + 作った (made; plain past form of 作る (to make)) + もので (because; since; for that reason; もので is a conjunctive particle that indicates a cause or reason; how to form: Verb (casual) + もので)]

本物そっくり look just like the real thing; realistic; authentic-looking [本物 (real thing; genuine article) + そっくり (just like; exactly like)]

です be; is

きっちょむさん、どう見ても Kicchomu, no matter how you look at it [きっちょむさん (Kicchomu) + どう見ても (no matter how you look at it; どう (how) + 見ても (from 見る (to see; to look; to view); ~ても means "no matter how ~" which is used when the opposite result happens (or opposite action is taken) to what people normally expected))]

私のネズミのほうが本物に見える my mouse looks more real (than yours) [私の (my; 私 (I; me) + の ('s; indicates possessive)) + ネズミ (mouse; rat) + のほうが (is more; conveys the idea that the noun it follows is "better" or "worse", "more" or "less", etc., depending on the sentence context; how to form: Noun + の + ほう + が) + 本物 (a real one; real thing; real stuff; genuine article) + に見える (to look; to appear; looks like; how to form: Noun + に見える)]

ぞ (sentence ender that adds force spoken by males)

首を横に振って shake (one's) head and [首 (head; neck) + を (indicates the direct object of action) + 横 (side-to-side; horizontal) + に (expresses direction) + 振って (shake and; て-form of 振る (to shake) which is used to connect to the next phrase, creating the meaning of "and")]

首を横に振ってこう言いました (Kicchomu) shook his head and said [首を横に振って (shook (his) head and) + こう (refers to what the speaker has said) + 言いました (said; polite past form of 言う (to say; to utter))]

「いいえ、私のネズミのほうが本物そっくりです。どうです？だれかに見せて、どちらが本物に見えるか、確かめましょう。」

「おお、それはいい考えだ。

いいえ no; nay

私のネズミのほうが本物そっくり my mouse looks more like the real thing [私の (my) + ネズミ (mouse; rat) + のほうが (is more; conveys the idea that the noun it follows is "better" or "worse", "more" or "less", etc., depending on the sentence context) + 本物 (a real one; real thing; real stuff; genuine article) + そっくり (just like; exactly like)]

です be; is

どうです？ what do you think?; how is it?

だれかに見せて show to someone and [だれか (someone; somebody) + に (to) + 見せて (show and; て-form of 見せる (to show; to display) which is used to connect to the next phrase; creating the meaning of "and")]

どちらが which is; which one [どちら (which one (especially of two alternatives)) + が (emphasizes the preceding word)]

本物に見えるか (which one) looks (more) real [本物 (real; a real one; real thing) + に見える (to look; to appear; looks like; how to form: Noun + に見える) + か (expresses the speaker's uncertainty about something)]

確かめましょう let's see [polite volitional form of 確かめる (to check; to make sure; to see; to ascertain); this verb form is used when the speaker suggests, urges, or initiates an act]

おお oh; ah

それは that is [それ (that; it) + は (indicates the sentence topic; adds emphasis)]

いい考え good idea [いい (good; agreeable; fine) + 考え (idea; plan; thought)]

だ be; is [casual form of the polite copula です (be; is)]

お寺の和尚さんに来ていただくかい？」「いえいえ、それよりも猫にお願いしましょう。猫なら、本物そっくりのネズミに飛びつくでしょう。」そこで、庄屋さんは猫を連れてきました。

お寺の和尚さん monk of the temple [お寺 (temple) + の (of; modifier) + 和尚さん (monk (especially the head monk of a temple); head priest; さん is a politeness marker which is used after a noun or sometimes な-adjective)]

お寺の和尚さんに来ていただく (we'll) have the monk of the temple come [お寺の和尚さん (monk of the temple) + に (expresses the object of the verb) + 来ていただく (have someone come; from 来る (to come); ~ていただく means "to have someone do something (humble/polite form)); 「person + に + Verb て-form + いただく」 means "to have a person do something for you"]

かい (strongly masculine sentence ending for asking questions) [is used for yes/no questions]

いえいえ no no; no

それよりも rather than that [それ (that; it) + よりも (rather than; in comparison to; more than ~)]

猫にお願いしましょう let's ask a cat [猫 (cat) + に (expresses the object of the verb) + お願いしましょう (let's ask; polite volitional form of お願いする (ask; request) which is used to make a suggestion to one or more people including oneself ("let's" / "shall we"))]

猫なら (I trust that) a cat (will ~) [猫 (cat) + なら (emphasizes the preceding word 猫; expresses one's ability or characteristic showing your trust)]

本物そっくりのネズミに飛びつくでしょう I'm sure (a cat) will jump at a mouse that looks just like the real thing [本物 (real thing; real stuff; genuine article) + そっくり (just like; exactly like) + の (modifier) + ネズミ (mouse; rat) + に (expresses the object of the verb) + 飛びつく (to jump at; to snatch) + でしょう (I'm sure; I believe; perhaps, I assume; is used to speculate based on your interpretation of something)]

そこで so; therefore; then

猫を連れてきました brought a cat [猫 (cat) + を (indicates the direct object of action) + 連れてきました (brought; polite past form of 連れてくる (bring; take along; fetch; get))]

猫(ねこ)の前(まえ)に、庄屋(しょうや)さんのネズミときっちょむさんのネズミを並(なら)べました。すると、猫(ねこ)は、庄屋(しょうや)さんのネズミには目(め)もくれず、きっちょむさんのネズミにぱっと飛(と)びつきました。

猫の前に in front of the cat [猫(ねこ) (cat) + の (of; modifier) + 前(まえ) (in front; before) + に (in; expresses the location of existence)]

庄屋さんのネズミ village headman's mouse [庄屋(しょうや)さん (village headman) + の ('s; of; modifier) + ネズミ (mouse; rat)]

と and

きっちょむさんのネズミ Kicchomu's mouse [きっちょむさん (Kicchomu) + の ('s; of; modifier) + ネズミ (mouse; rat)]

並べました arranged in a line [polite past form of 並(なら)べる (to arrange in a line; to line up; to set up)]

すると then; and; thereupon [can be used to begin a sentence or clause]

庄屋さんのネズミには目もくれず without a look at the village headman's mouse [庄屋(しょうや)さんのネズミ (village headman's mouse) + には (puts more emphasis and restriction on the preceding word) + 目(め)もくれず (without a look at; without a glance; taking no notice; ~ず means "without doing")]

きっちょむさんのネズミにぱっと飛びつきました suddenly jumped at Kicchomu's mouse [きっちょむさんのネズミ (Kicchomu's mouse) + に (expresses the object of the verb) + ぱっと (suddenly; in a flash; rapidly) + 飛(と)びつきました (jumped at; polite past form of 飛(と)びつく (to jump at; to be attracted by))]

実(じつ)は、きっちょむさんのネズミは、かつお節(ぶし)で作(つく)ってあったのです。

おしまい。

猫実(じつ)は truth to tell; the thing is; in reality; as a matter of fact [実 (truth; reality) + は (adds emphasis)]

きっちょむさんのネズミは Kicchomu's mouse [きっちょむさん (Kicchomu) + の ('s; of; modifier) + ネズミ (mouse; rat) + は (indicates the sentence topic)]

かつお節(ぶし)で作(つく)ってあった was made of dried bonito [かつお節 (dried bonito fish; slab of dried bonito) + で (by; with; of) + 作ってあった (was made (intentionally); from 作(つく)る (to make); ~てあった is the plain past form of ~てある (is used when the result of an intentional action still affects the current state, or the result exists until the moment when the speaker describes it); how to form: Verb て-form + あった)]

のです can say with confidence that...; it is assuredly that ...

おしまい the end

Kicchomu's Mouse Carving

Please try to tackle the Japanese first and use this only as needed.

Once upon a time, there was an interesting man named Kicchomu.

One day, the village headman called Kicchomu to his house. The village headman was rich and always did nothing but brag, so Kicchomu didn't like him very much. The village headman happily started bragging again when Kicchomu came.

"I recently asked a great master at carving to make this for me", he said and brought out a carving of a mouse. "See, this mouse looks just like it's alive, doesn't it?", he said and grinned. Kicchomu stared at the mouse carving and said, "Village Headman, this mouse is certainly well-made. But I can make a better one. I'll make and show it to you by tomorrow."

The next day, Kicchomu went to the village headman's house with the mouse carving he had made and showed it to the village headman. Kicchomu's mouse which he made overnight, was ugly and didn't look like a mouse at all. On the other hand, the village headman's mouse looked just like the real thing, since it was made by a master.

"Kicchomu, no matter how you look at it, my mouse looks more real than yours."

Kicchomu shook his head and said, "No, my mouse looks more like the real thing.

"What do you think? Let's show these to someone and see which one looks more real."

"Oh, that's a good idea. We'll have the monk of the temple come?"

"No, no. Let's ask a cat rather than that. I'm sure a cat will jump at a mouse that looks just like the real thing."

So, the village headman brought a cat. The village headman's mouse and Kicchomu's mouse were arranged in front of the cat. Then, the cat suddenly jumped at Kicchomu's mouse without a look at the village headman's mouse.

Truth be told, Kicchomu's mouse was made of dried bonito fish.

The End.

きっちょむさんのネズミの彫り物

むかしむかし、きっちょむさんという面白い人がいました。

ある日、庄屋さんがきっちょむさんを家に呼びました。庄屋さんは、お金持ちでいつも自慢ばかりしているので、きっちょむさんは庄屋さんのことがあまり好きではありません。庄屋さんは、きっちょむさんが来ると、嬉しそうにまた自慢話を始めました。

「最近、たいへんな彫り物の名人にお願いして、これをつくってもらったよ。」と言って、出してきたのは、ネズミの彫り物でした。「ほら、このネズミは、まるで、生きているみたいだろう？」と言って、にやにやしています。

きっちょむさんは、ネズミの彫り物をじっと見てから、こう言いました。「庄屋さん、確かにこのネズミはよくできています。でも、私はもっとうまく作れます。明日までに作ってお見せしましょう。」

次の日、きっちょむさんは、自分で作ったネズミの彫り物を持って庄屋さんの家に行きました。そして、庄屋さんに自分の作ったネズミの彫り物を見せました。一晩で作ったきっちょむさんのネズミは不細工で、どう見てもネズミには見えません。一方、庄屋さんのネズミは、名人が作ったもので、本物そっくりです。

「きっちょむさん、どう見ても私のネズミのほうが本物に見えるぞ。」きっちょむさんは、首を横に振ってこう言いました。

「いいえ、私のネズミのほうが本物そっくりです。どうです？だれかに見せて、どちらが本物に見えるか、確かめましょう。」

「おお、それはいい考えだ。お寺の和尚さんに来ていただくかい？」

「いえいえ、それよりも猫にお願いしましょう。猫なら、本物そっくりのネズミに飛びつくでしょう。」

そこで、庄屋さんは猫を連れてきました。猫の前に、庄屋さんのネズミときっちょむさんのネズミを並べました。すると、猫は、庄屋さんのネズミには目もくれず、きっちょむさんのネズミにぱっと飛びつきました。

実は、きっちょむさんのネズミは、かつお節で作ってあったのです。

おしまい。

Kanji in Focus

It is usually helpful to create a story based on the meanings of the kanji parts. Often, different kanji learning systems will use different "meanings" for the parts. We try to give the most common ones, but consistency is best. Choose one meaning per kanji part and stick with it. The following are a selection of the kanji found in this story. The underlined reading is probably the most used.

慢	READINGS MEANING EXAMPLE	マン ridicule; laziness 自慢 (じまん) pride; boast	忄 heart 日 sun; day 罒 net 又 again; once more; once again Without *laziness* of the **heart** 忄, work hard under the **sun** 日 to restore this fishing **net** 罒 **again** 又.
彫	READINGS MEANING EXAMPLE	チョウ・ほる・~ぼり carve; engrave; chisel 彫り物 (ほりもの) carving; engraving; sculpture	冂 upside down box 土 soil; earth; dirt; mud 口 mouth; opening; hole; gap 彡 stylized three; hair After removing the **upside down box** 冂, we found a *chisel* covered with **dirt** 土 inside a **hole** 口 filled with corn **hair** 彡.
作	READINGS MEANING EXAMPLE	サク・サ・つくる・つくり・~づくり make; production; prepare; build 作る (つく) to make; to produce	亻 person; man; human 𠂉 person 丨 line; vertical stroke 一 one; horizontal stroke A **man** 亻 who *prepares* to become a **person** 𠂉 who will excel in the **line** 丨 of his profession, is **one** 一 of a kind.
猫	READINGS MEANING EXAMPLE	ビョウ・ねこ cat 子猫 (こねこ) kitten	犭 dog; tail 艹 grass; herb 田 field; rice field A **dog** 犭 is chasing a *cat* towards a **grass** 艹 **field** 田.
尚	READINGS MEANING EXAMPLE	ショウ・なお esteem; furthermore; still; yet 和尚 (おしょう) monk; head priest	丨 line; vertical stroke 丷 sparks 冋 desert; border prairie He checks the power **line** 丨 that *still* **sparks** 丷 in the middle of the **desert** 冋.

Kanji in Focus Continued

節	READINGS MEANING EXAMPLE	セツ・セチ・ふし・~ぶし・のっと node; season; period; tune; verse; joint かつお節(ぶし) small pieces of sliced dried bonito	竹 bamboo 即 instantly; at once; immediately While it's sill the growing *season* of **bamboo 竹**, plant **immediately 即**.
飛	READINGS MEANING EXAMPLE	ヒ・とぶ・とばす・~とばす fly; skip (pages); scatter 飛(と)びつく to jump at; to be attracted by	飞 fly 丨 line; vertical stroke 亻 person; man; human 飞 fly They *scatter* the balloons to **fly 飞** high above that **line 丨** near the **person 亻** who is holding a **fly 飞** rod.
細	READINGS MEANING EXAMPLE	サイ・ほそい・ほそる・こまか・こまかい narrow; slender; detailed; get thin 不細工(ぶさいく) ugly; poorly made; unattractive	糸 thread; yarn; string 田 field; rice field Pass a *narrow* road to locate the **thread 糸** of gold in the hidden **field 田**.
持	READINGS MEANING EXAMPLE	ジ・もつ・~もち・もてる hold; have お金持(かねも)ち rich; rich person	扌 hand 土 soil; earth; dirt; mud 寸 length; measurement We *have* friends who lend a **hand 扌** to help us clean the **dirt 土** and measure the **length 寸** of our garden.
実	READINGS MEANING EXAMPLE	ジツ・シツ・み・みのる・まこと・みの・みちる reality; truth 事実(じじつ) fact; truth; reality	宀 roof 三 three 人 person; people; man In *reality*, this **roof 宀** needs to be repaired by **three 三 people 人**.

Do you have any questions? Anything confusing? Feel free to email me (Clay) at clay@thejapanshop.com with any questions, comments, or suggestions.

Do you have ideas to make *Makoto* better? We'd love to hear from you. Did something particularly help you? Love to hear that as well.

What to experience even more Makoto? Learn about our new Makoto+ membership. Download the latest issue or access web-based back issues. All this and more starting at only $3. Go to: **www.MakotoPlus.com** now!

Clay & Yumi

www.ingramcontent.com/pod-product-compliance
Ingram Content Group UK Ltd.
Pitfield, Milton Keynes, MK11 3LW, UK
UKHW061828190726
13853UKWH00009B/2500

9 798408 575718